Wait & See

poems by
Dylan Lucas *Snaman*

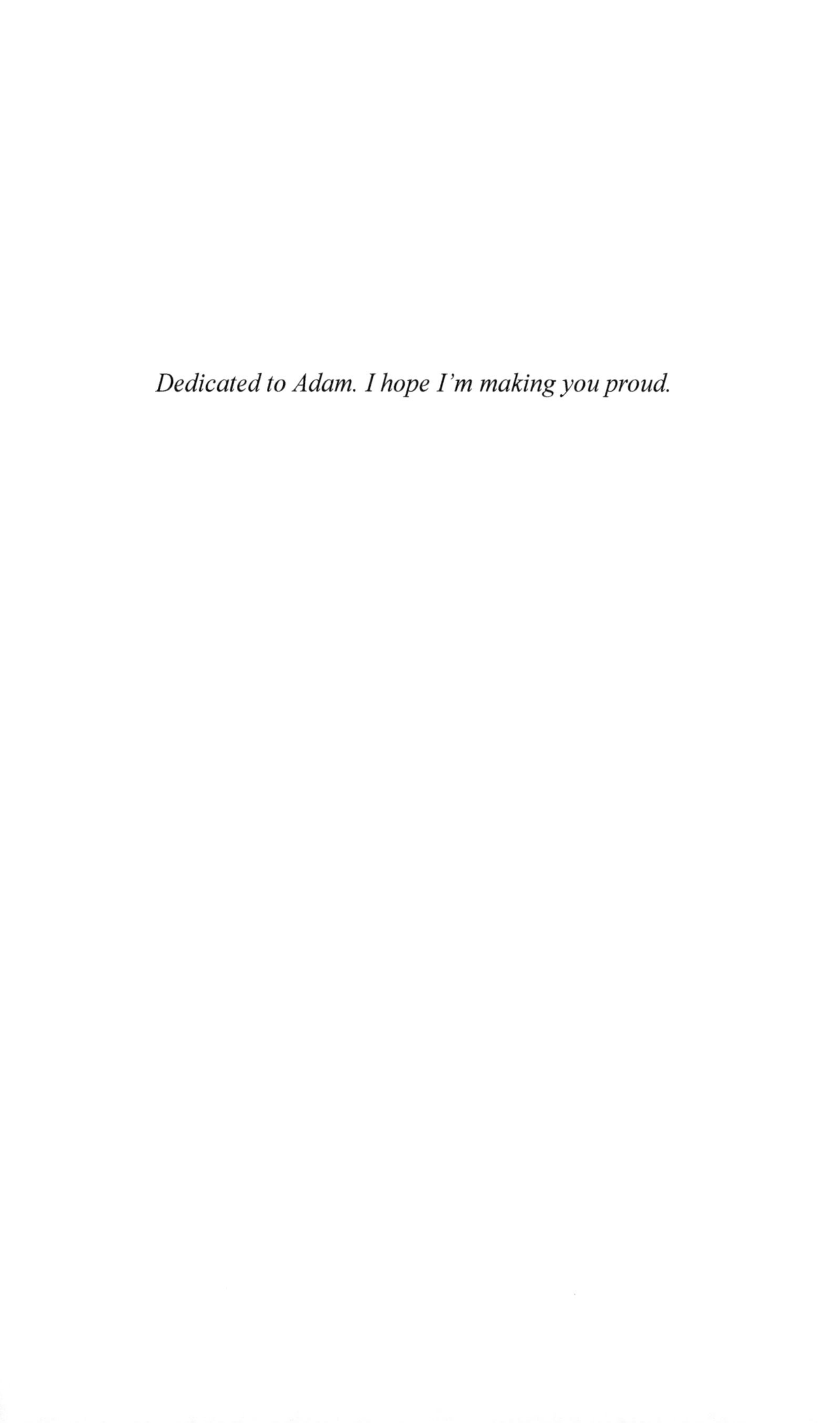

Dedicated to Adam. I hope I'm making you proud.

Table of Contents

Welcome, friend. I hope this book finds you well. Figuring out the best way to arrange all my thoughts has been as much of a journey as the one it took to write all the poems themselves; Well…almost. I hope you enjoy your time here but more than anything, I want you to know that whatever journey you're on, be it mental health, medical trouble or something I myself haven't experienced, you have a friend in me. In my life, there have been times where I've felt like the statue in the town square everyone stops to admire on a sunny afternoon, but there have also been times when I have felt like the dried up wad of gum stuck beneath its feet.

Over these next however many pages, I hope to make you feel something you haven't known in a long time, be it remembering the face of an old friend or simply, and most importantly, a smile. Thank you for taking the time to listen to what stories I have to share. I hope you hear something you like.

Poetry in my heart feels like a security blanket.
A shield from the frostbite of a world that's slowly freezing
to death.

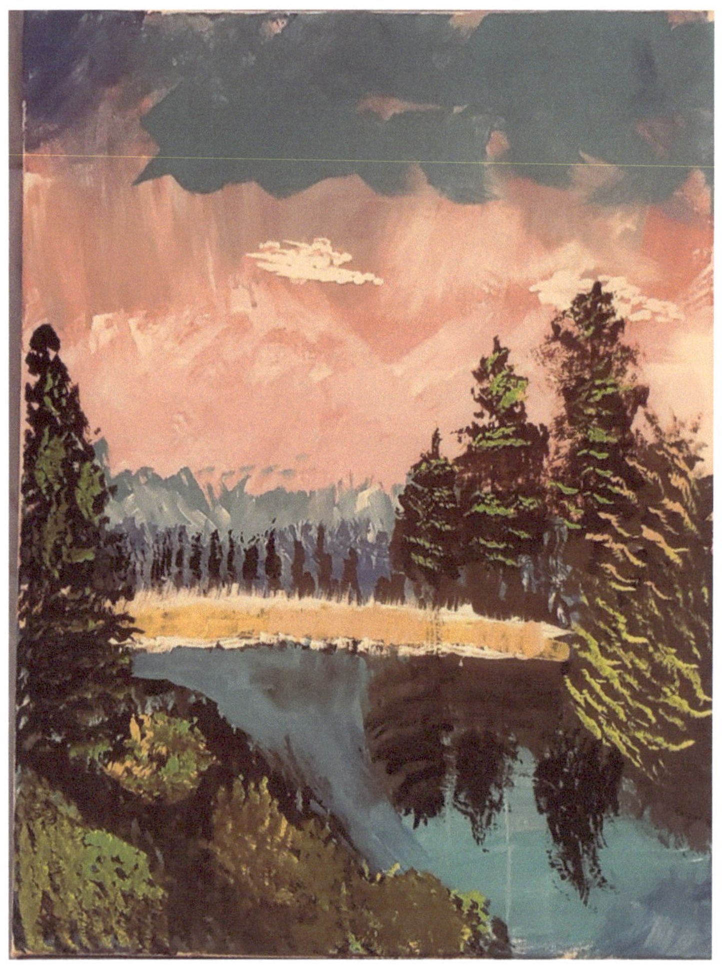

A college professor once told me, "Man isn't built to
comprehend the riddles of time."
Well that may be true,
but I can try.

Tinder (but not that kind.)

In our fridge, my parents keep the eggs on top of their
cigarettes.
So if you want to start your day off right,
you have to move the stupid eggs out of the way first.

But really, when I think about the good ol' days,
I remember my mother's clothes, how they always smelled
of smoke. From the time I was a toddler riding bitch in the
backseat of our '95 cutlass supreme, all the way to middle
school chorus class, I knew the other kids were looking at
me funny.

"Why do you smell like that?"

Great, nobody here even knows my name but now
everyone just knows me as "that kid who always smells
bad."
I suppose over time you grow accustomed to it. I hadn't
noticed the stench coming from my Spiderman lunchbox or
the taste it left in my PB&J, minus the PB (I was a weird
kid,) I just remembered my mother's hands. Tired from
raising 3 boys since all the way back in the '70's but still
soft, like when the doctor says they got the scans back and
we need to come in right away.

When I went in for surgery, she rushed home and made
sure to grab my teddy bear so I'd have it when I woke up. I
still have that bear to this day, named Teddy (not the most
creative name, I'll admit.) I hold him close every now and
then, and what do you know, even after all these years,

I still smell smoke.

Ember
=====

A blue flame burns bright
despite the shadows dancing along the kitchen tile.
Hurricanes and monsoons
begging
to terminate its shine,
but a ceasefire was nowhere to be found.

I like to believe it's still glowing bright
somewhere
keeping somebody warm.

<u>To Christina</u>

I skid my knee the day I stumbled upon your name
and the scar it left is my favorite memory.

Before you became a memory, I'd sing your name into the
ceiling fan like a little kid,
just because I loved the way it sounded.
You taught us how to make a home out of ourselves;
That it was okay to be a little weird even if we would never
know the warmth of a Crowded Room because of it.
Your smile rings in my ears and I Think of You,
the way you believed in the world
or the love notes you left on its windowsill.

They say you should never meet your Heroes.
Maybe that's because they don't think anyone could live up
to the portraits we paint in our heads,
but the only surprise when we met was how much taller
than you I was.
I racked my brain for any resemblance of the English
language but failed to report back.
You told me I was sweet and gave me a hug.
That's when I finally understood;
It's not the sound of the song that matters,
only the one singing it.

I keep a dusty concert ticket in my dresser drawer
and hold it like a trophy medal;
a memento of a girl who set the world on fire,
even if it was only 'til 22.
That's 22 reasons more to spread joy in the world
and meet every new heart
With Love.

<u>Growth</u>

1.
Flesh rips in two
as a tricycle wheel stays spinning in the air.
Why there was dirt piled high next to the bus stop
that we decided to make into a ramp, I couldn't tell you, but

gravity

has a way of making you wish you could sprout wings
to avoid the concrete's awful embrace,
'cause we all know he gives the worst hugs in the world.
Mom brings me inside and makes some cinnamon toast
to calm me down.
Sweet dreams are made of this.

2.
Mom and Dad were on their honeymoon the first time
the pain started,
and so I became pretty familiar with the school nurse's
office.
I don't like that picture there,
and what if you moved that mirror to the other side?
I don't like staring at myself here in shambles.
Her only remedies to my cries were dark rooms
beige pedestals
and cold glasses of tap water.
Bless her heart.
The chiropractor thought she could squeeze the ache from
my tissues,
bending and twisting my body like a pretzel at the
fair.
Even when I could not turn my head to meet her gaze
or raise my hand to shake hers,

she always had my back.
The wise words of our family doctor stated that it was
all in my head,
that I just missed my parents.
"Quit being so dramatic,
Give it a week and you won't even remember any of this
happened."

Thank God for Doctor Dan,
what would the family do without him?

3.
A locomotive trudges towards the finish line
of the second grade spelling bee.
I look out into the audience and see your prideful grin.
I see you cheering me on.
I see you telling your best friends about my triumph
over the time bomb
tick
tick
ticking in my head.
I see you canceling your trip to Pittsburgh
so I have someone there to
keep me company.
I see you watching me like an eagle watches her fledgling
inch closer and
closer
towards the deadly kiss of the asphalt,
praying
that he learns to spread his wings
before he's just another foul memory.

ICU nurses came to know me better than I knew myself
most days,
my head determined to turn itself inside out.

Hospital clowns' jokes seem to
never land
when you're 6 years old and picking out a birthday cake
in the shape of a headstone.

Even now,
the stench of MRI contrast,
like notes of expired Vick's vapor rub,
makes me feel like I'm back driving along the peaks and
valleys of the heart monitor
praying for a safe trip home.

4.
The doctor calls and says the cyst is growing again.
Spreading like peanut butter on a graham cracker or
cinnamon on toast.
"It's no big deal," she says.
They just have to put a catheter in my brain to help drain
the cyst.

You've been through worse in the past.
Quit being so dramatic.
Give it a few weeks and you'll be back to
normal,
like none of this ever happened.

I guess Doctor Dan was right.
After all these years,
It really was
all in my head.

<u>Scratches</u>

In my chest sits a record player, surrounded
by an infinite number of shelves and bookcases
housing the soundtrack to my every memory
on 7-track vinyl sets.

Grab the first one you see and press play. Revel
in the bounce and dip of the piano
or the cool sway of the trumpet man.
Think Ellington-style swing,
that kind of itch in the sole of your shoe only a two-step
can soothe.
Groove to the beat even though you look as out of place
as whiskey neat in champagne glasses.
Summer nights rockin' to the rhythm
as we roam through the city we grew up in, uncovering
hidden gems beneath the crust of our hometown.
Dirt path painted by the shimmers of midday,
A plate of the best mozzarella sticks you've ever had
from a main street cafe,
or the friendly stranger in the corner of the bar you'll likely
never see again
after tonight.

Pause.

Take the record off the needle and place it back on the
shelf.
Handle with care,
that way the trumpets still ring as bright the next time you
sing along.
You never want to forget the words to your favorite tune.

Cabin walls of chocolate begin to melt

as the fireplace makes its presence known like a
lion screaming its name into the Serengeti. A beast
of a storm is raging beyond these walls but
we are safe,
tucked away under pillow forts in our parents' basement.
Sweet lullabies swirl around our heads
as echoes from the flute ring
like a train whistle
barreling through the night.
You've spent a century encased in a block of ice,
frostbitten by dreams buried underground
and thank you letters never sent.
Let the fireplace hold you in its arms
and melt away the igloo you built around yourself
to keep out the cold.

You sink deeper and deeper
into your mother's futon as the stereo's siren song
paints the room in a grainy haze,
giving a whole new meaning to the word
"melody."
"Hallelujah"
traipses along my tongue
as the flute sings us to sleep.

Sings us to
Sings us
Sings

Ever since we said our last
goodbyes,
Heaving cigar smoke in your pickup truck
gazing out across the highway,
this record refuses to play.
It's almost like it knows
I won't like the song it has to sing.

I cut my tongue on the last words you spoke
and sing them in a round
beside your open casket.
The coroners say you drifted off
humming Schubert as you took your
final bow.
Now I sing Ave Maria to an empty room
as I remember the friend
I didn't deserve.

<u>I Love to Sing</u>

Ask anyone who has spent more than an afternoon with me.
My voice is one of my most prized possessions.
When we were in elementary school, waiting for the school
bus to take us home, the other kids would pretend I was a
jukebox. They'd sit me on a desk, call out random songs
and I would belt them out into the chalkboard. You'd be
hard-pressed to find a time of day when I wasn't making
some kind of noise. Be it the backseat of my mom's
Mitsubishi or the dugout of our little league game, I would
turn the space into center stage at Carnegie Hall. It didn't
matter to me if no one came out to the show; music was
just my thing. Then the diagnosis came.
Now I sing into the mirror and get only dust clouds in
return.
They tell me the medicine will bring me back to normal but
they failed to mention what pill I should take to get my
voice back. Maybe the magic tablet spilled down the drain
while I wasn't looking. Rest assured, I will twist my arms
until they hiss at the bottom of the septic system if that's
what it takes.
Please.
I just want to feel like me again.

Slumber

I've heard it said that Sleep is Death's cousin.
Maybe that's why I find it so hard to get out of bed in the
morning.

But it would make more sense if Dreams
were invited to that family potluck too.
A Dream is like Sleep's clingy little brother,
always clutching by his side.
So if Sleep and Death are like two kids
wrestling beneath the Christmas tree before sunrise,
then it would stand to reason,
through the transitive property,
that the visions of snowy mountain peaks and
the red sands of Mars in between my toes
have brought me here
to the glowing doorway standing before me.
The omen of the surrounding pinstriped walls
planted wasps in my stomach,
swelling my throat with every word I never had the guts to
say.

I push past the point of no return
fleeing from every fantasy that has followed me through
my loneliest restless night.
I spit up a gallon of water from my 12-year-old lungs
and shake hands with a sailor man,
withered away by centuries past,
now no more than a pile of bones,
hollow and bare.
I hurl myself into this ocean of
the unknown
and gasp for air as I sink down to the very bed of my
despair.

Just then, a sea serpent shrouded in a cloud of pixie dust
kisses me on the cheek and whispers

"time to go."

I wake upon the ceiling,
my lungs filling with helium.
I wave goodbye to photos of cabins in the snow
as I slip out of my bedroom window
and rest upon the branch of a weeping willow.
My eyelids collapse under the pressure of the
moon
and as they meet,
the organ sounds.

The Very First Time I Went Crowdsurfing

He was carried along by the crowd.
Like ocean waves they moved him along the masses.
If only he could have found his footing
on his own,
but at least he was actually going somewhere new
for once.

<u>Haunted</u>

Forgive me for this one, Nunna.

Maybe instead of heaven or hell,
you are reincarnated as the smallest bug you ever stepped
on.
Beetle for some, a whole ant hill for others.

The ghost ant is an insect so small they are hardly visible to
the naked eye.
Simply touching them pushes the air right out of their tiny
little bodies,
leaving them lying still in the summer sun.

There we sat, seven years old,
drinking apple juice on our neighbor's patio and
testing the wonders of the natural world.
It was so fascinating how these tiny little bugs would
die
from the slightest touch.

Maybe in the next life, the world is nothing more than a
flower garden,
bigger than the entire world we once knew.
It's pretty calm here, nice shade from all the plants around.
But every now and then,
these monsters fresh out of Eden come and visit.
Oh no, watch out!
A finger!

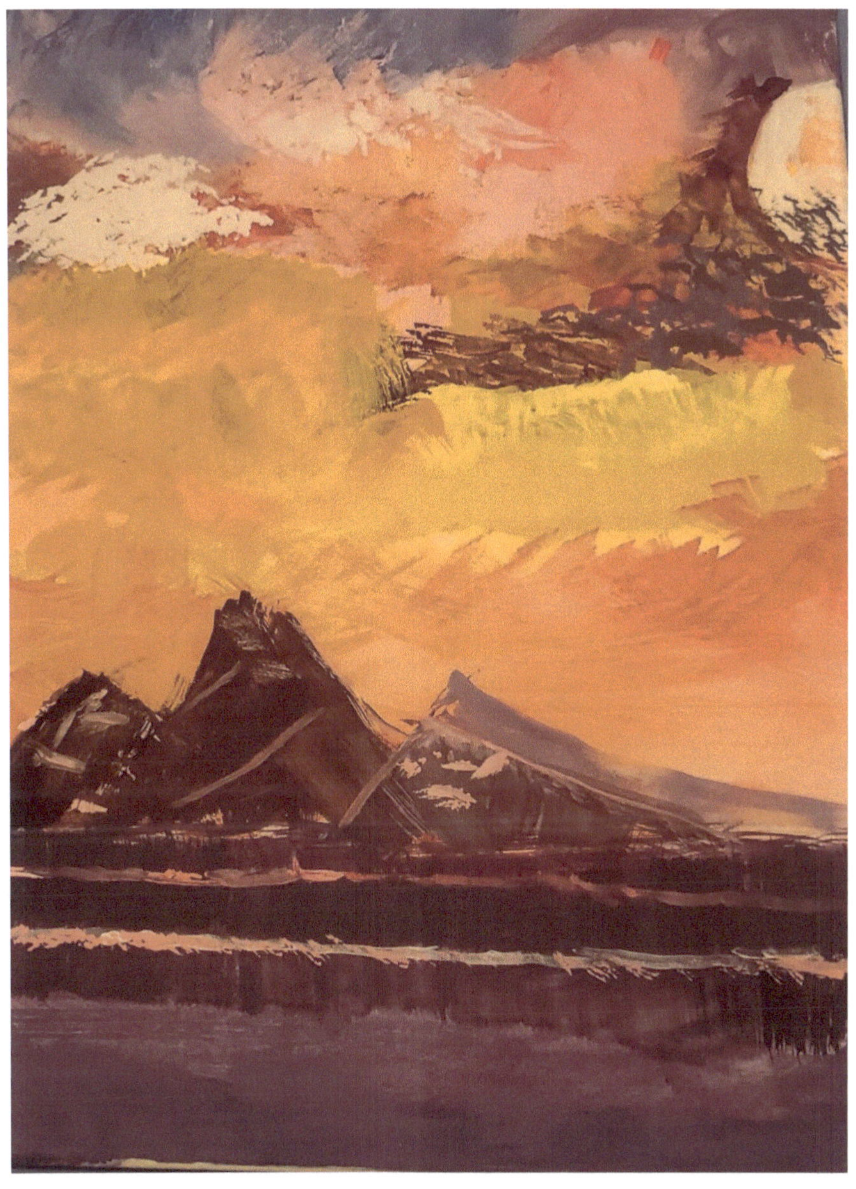

<u>Stranger</u>

Hey, where did you come from?
I'm so damn forgetful,
I must have left the door open by mistake
and lost the key.

The reality of you escapes me.
it's like the monsters under my bed and the skeletons in my
closet
spent one drunken night in the city,
had a little too much fun,
and you are their
sick
twisted
offspring.
You're like the worst movie theatre in history.
You only play the pictures in my head that I've spent a
lifetime
trying to forget.

I've called the landlord more times than I can count
to come and change these damn locks already
but somehow,
you keep getting in.

<u>Claustrophobic</u>

There is too much chaos here for order to abide.
Thoughts like a speed train,
bound to collide.
Peace treaties discarded and tossed to the side.
Here, awake at midnight, eyes open wide.

it wasn't always so crowded here.
There used to be loads of space reserved for
our favorite restaurants and the summer Tommy got sick
from eating too much saltwater taffy.

but this space was renovated years ago and now
those days are gathered up, packed away and slid to a
dark
dusty
corner of the attic.

Fear and doubt moved in years ago,
and now they're the noisiest tenants in the building,
rattling the walls the moment we retire for the night.

I wish I had some place else to live,
but this is the only home I've ever known.

<u>Sinking</u>

The day the bottom gave out
is the day I learned to tread water.
Tell me the story's over
and I'll write you a new one.
Years of rain have left this smile weary and wilted,
but I'm still standing tall
even as the thunder swells around me.

Get me out of this hospital room.
Please.
I miss my bed.
All these nurses turned private-eye investigators
searching the premises for a corpse every hour
on the hour
are making it feel like I'm already a ghost in this place
wandering the halls.

I won't lie,
these legs don't work like they used to,
but dammit,
I've played double-dutch with the devil in his school of
forgotten misfits my entire life
and I haven't tripped yet.

Call my words melted.
Call them blurry.
Call them what you want but
they are finally my own.

Eight times you've fashioned me into a jack-o-lantern
and eight times I've lit up the night sky
making music the only way I know how,
scraping my heart onto canvas,
hoping someone can find solace in the bruises.

As a kid, I used to have this recurring nightmare where I
drowned in a riptide.
No matter how close to the shore I would get,
the waves would swaddle me back in their arms every time.
I cough up cat collars and concert tapes as I sink beneath
the surface,
The memory of me no more
than just a footprint in the sand.

It was always at this point that I would wake up,
Except now.

A hand plunges beneath the water and drags me back
towards the shore.
Air rushes back into my lungs like a gunshot
as I look toward this kind stranger.
I want to thank them for saving me, but realize
the hand is my own.
You crash my sandcastle
but I will be here, always, to build it back up again,
shovel and pale in hand.

I set my knapsack on the kitchen counter
and part the curtains to let in the light.
A while I've been away,
so I will take this urn of roses and make potpourri.
Dust the vases trapped in the cabinet and fill them with
lavender.
Out of my bag I find a painting of some kind I must have
picked up at the beach. It's not perfect but I like the way it
looks on the front door, how its red edges burn brightest
just as the sun goes down;
The way that it twinkles when the air is still.

It doesn't feel like the home I once knew,
but I'd much rather live in a place like this.

<u>Happy Holidays!</u>

We always have fun at Mr. Jack's house.
He always has the best stories to tell.
Like one time, he spent the entire summer living inside his
backyard treehouse.
Come hell or hurricane,
he never went back inside.
The time he watched the streetlights flicker all the way 'til
dawn
until he had to get ready for his shift at the marina,
mooring boats to the dock;
About his brother who never made it out of rehab,
unable to tie him down, despite all the interventions.

Flashbacks of Christmas Day
flutter along the drive-in theatre of my mind.
I can almost smell our holiday feast
resting on azure tablecloth.
The men in my family crowd around a deep fryer,
trading war stories.
My uncle in Korea,
me in the pediatric unit.
The timer dings ready and we pull up a turkey,
golden brown and ready to dig into.
I wish I could say it was the only time
we took comfort around a corpse,
but what says "I love you"
more than a belly, full,
and clammy hands, joined in prayer?

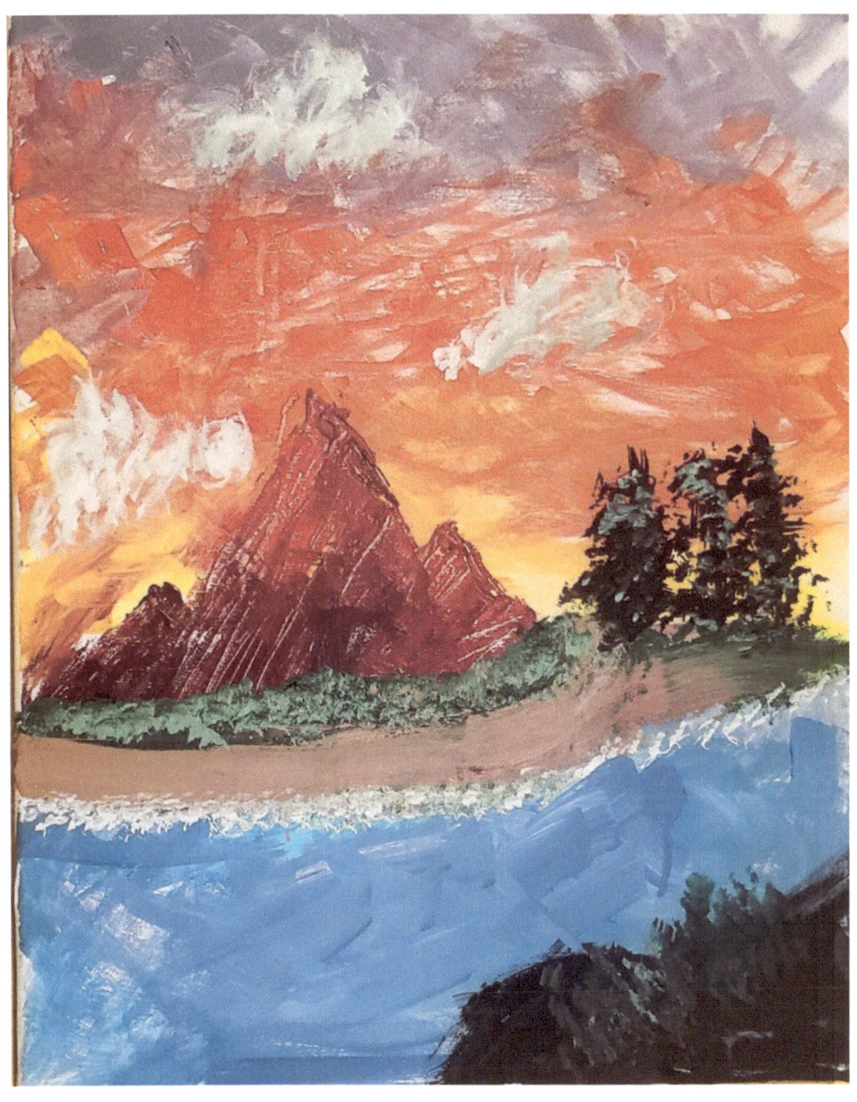

Nice to Meet You
<u> </u>

An empty plate of onion rings.
A wine glass stumbling to its feet.
The off-white tablecloth we sat as we watched
the evening rain
over the factories of Chicago.
The story about your grandmother who left home when she
was seventeen
and the galaxies painted across your skin.
Just how many times you've had to call
your second cousin to come pick you up from the bus stop
at 3am.

A lonely cab ride.
The samba of lock and key
revealing a twin size mattress
wrapped in slated bed sheets.
the flicker of 3am Full House reruns
and a table meant for two.

Mirror

Who am I?
Am I the suitcase,
neatly packed and ready for the trip?
Or am I the lonely stranger
sitting by themselves in the corner of the cafe
writing a poem?
My ego likes to believe the former,
but really,
I don't know the answers either.

Some days,
I feel like I am just a pool float,
drifting along at the mercy of the tide.
Other days, I am the ship,
commanding the sea.

I am a scribble on the page,
making it up as I go.

<u>Muddy</u>

a lonely day, only not so
lonely.

Here I sit,
the sun gently beaming on marks of beavers on ash.
Nothing but the soft breeze
and the crinkles of water passing by.
A hawk cries in the distance, searching
for his afternoon snack.
Fallen trees litter my path,
a sign of years past.
On this day, I am at peace.

I am beginning to learn the value
in being content in one's own company.

Twilight

Stars make the perfect party guests,
always bearing gifts.
Fully equipped with ghost stories by the campfire or
champagne by sangria-sheened shoreline.
Remember our midnight treks down the interstate?
Driving fast enough to make death feel like
just another fairytale our parents made up to keep us from
staying out too late?
We swore those days would never end,
but the twinkle in your eye seared through the cozy of my
cardigan
leaving me frozen in the snow.

Now, Venus is my only companion here
as I ponder thoughts that I will never know the answers to.
If I dove headfirst into a black hole,
swimming trunks and all,
would I land in your arms?
What if light decided to stop and smell the roses?
Would I even be writing this?
I hang my head for all the stars never deemed
worthy enough
for a name.
A pretty memory of what once was
the center of a whole galaxy,
now no more than just a shimmer in the night sky,
dim and distant.

I've spent many a restless night
scrubbing away the sound of your smile,
but the echoes of your name still haunt the walls of this
lonely place.

<u>Rising</u>

It's probably been years since I've sipped coffee with the
morning crescent moon.
But when my cat greeted me hello
like an impatient alarm clock at 5:47am,
I did not hit snooze.
Instead,
I filled her bowl with crunchies,
grabbed a coat,
and listened
to the morning greet me with open arms.

The air conditioner is humming
louder than a stranger on the subway,
this pen has yet to join me here, constantly running out
of ink,
and my toes are conspiring against the cold,
but the sky is as blue as a metaphor
I haven't found the words to yet and the birds
sing like they're just happy to have an audience.

Maybe it's not some grand revelation.
Simply
the ability to say
"I am here."

<u>Cozy</u>

Take me back to honeysuckle summer times.
Days so sweet, we could catch a sugar rush
just by running through the sprinkler system.
My mother used to spend all her free time knitting,
weaving silk together like a conductor at the philharmonic.
Whenever I'd get scared, the blankie she made would
remind me that love could never leave my side.

Mrs. Amber is my mom's best friend,
and besides a 2-3 year period where they didn't speak,
almost every weekend was spent at her house.
The little boy in me loved watching cheddar cheese melt
on crackers in her microwave, never knowing that his head
would follow suit in just a few years' time.

She taught me a lot, like how to make a Cobb salad.
And as the years passed, she egged me on
to try (and fail) to ride a bike,
and get my first job,
and drive a car,
and picked me up when I totaled that car.

Now,
we toast wine glasses as we play games of Uno,
and she beats me every time.
I remember one time when I was six, I flipped my big
wheel in her front yard
and she was there
to scrape me off the driveway
like egg burnt on a frying pan.

I met one of the first girls I ever loved at Mrs. Amber's
house.
And on cool summer nights, we'd set up tents in her
backyard together and gaze up at the sky's yesterdays.
Our makeshift campsite kept us safe from any monsters
hiding in the dark
and we traded ghost stories just to prove how
unafraid we were.

I could see the entire world from the top of an oak tree,
and everything was
Okay.

Rewind

Ah, the majesty of the second chance.
To know the charity of the do-over.
How different things would be if we could just
go back and flip the script
like the director for the musical we performed in high
school.
How she would make us rehearse our dance routines
blindfolded,
just to make sure we weren't peeking to our castmates for
help.
Her methods may have been a little unorthodox,
but by the end, we put on the best damn show
that auditorium had ever seen.

This time,
maybe you just stay home.
You were never good at driving in the rain,
so call the office and just tell them you're not coming in
today.
We can watch a movie on the couch like we used to.
You want pretzels or popcorn?
Take what you want and come sit next to me.
I know you don't like mob movies as much as I do,
but there's just something about that world, you know?
Family-
what a glorious thing to lose.

This time,
instead of the bottle,
pick up the phone.
Give me a call.
I promise to listen until
the voices let you fall asleep.

Just promise you'll call me back in the morning.
Maybe you never move out west,
and we go for more of those bookstore trips you loved
so much.
Take as much time as you need,
we have an eternity to wait.

This time, I cancel the house party.
I never find you on the storage room floor
and there's no fateful backseat to the vet that I can't be a
part of.
We spend your last day here,
together,
and just take a nap on the sofa like we used to.

You were the best welcoming party a guy could ask for.
What I wouldn't give for just
one last surprise.

<u>Wake Up</u>   2018

I've never been one to say much about how I feel
but over the years, the situation got too real.
Late nights and
hate
light the last eight years.
Fate might just take flight
if I don't face fears.
But,
The monster in the mirror is me.
I'm staring at him,
trying, 'cause I'm dying
to see.
Whatever happened to the person,
that guy that I used to be?
He must have got lost
along the way while trying to flee.
Like, "Which way should I go?'

Hey man, I don't know.
I go through every day not knowing who's friend
or foe.
Like an age-long setup with no ending to the joke,
I gotta get out of the flames 'fore it all goes up in
smoke.

So,
I'm still trying my best.
Still try to get out of bed every day and try to get dressed.
Even through it all, my heart still beats in my chest
With all this stress, I guess I just need a
deep
rest.

Yes,
My message is true.
Oftentimes,
I wish I could be alone in the room.
Life is like a movie,
I'm just trying to do it all on cue.
Here's to hoping someday soon that I won't be
singing the blues.

Stop Suffering to Make Yourself Feel Better

I couldn't make it out of bed this morning.
I only got two hours of sleep last night.
I haven't left my house in over a month and
I've forgotten what my Nunna's living room smells like.

For as long as I can remember,
I've wanted to be poetic.
My words need to have a purpose.
If I'm not making lyrics out of my grocery list,
Then the moment is already spoiled
If my stroll around the neighborhood can't double as a
metaphor for childhood,
no one will want to read about it.

Who am I kidding, (Get it?)
the only way to write is to
suffer.
Suffocate on your own saliva
so that someone else can call it
inspired.
Break down at the weekend barbecue
so that the neighbors can tell
you're back to your old self again.
People want art. Not an autobiography.

Do your part, give us something to dance to.

But earlier today, I opened a box of letters from my
preschoolers saying how much they
miss me
and all the games they want to play when I
Finally
come home.
They didn't ask for a new story,

or a fresh set of knock-knock jokes.
They just miss Mr. Dylan.

One time while I was handing out breakfast,
one of my students told me I was a superhero
and I almost cried.
I don't think there is any greater achievement in this world
than to be a superhero in the eyes of a three-year-old.

This morning, my cat woke me up by nudging her face
against my own.
I'll call that poetry.
Today I counted an extra french fry in my Wendy's bag.
I'll call that poetry.
Last week, my grandmother called me at the crack of dawn
to tell me there was a show on TV she thought I'd like.
If that's not poetic, then I don't know what is.

This is a promise to you
and me,
that I will stop drowning myself in an attempt to seem
enlightened.
You know why?
Because grapes and clementines are fucking delicious
and I have a lot more of them that I want to try.

Brave

My biggest fear?
The day the trees stop singing.
That one day, I wake up and there's no laughter left
to sprinkle into my morning coffee.
When the storm threatens to toss me under the dirt,
the earthworms and I sing lullabies
until my alarm clock digs me out of the ground.

The closest I came to the end
was the day my feet moonlit as crabs in the sand
ducking for cover,
barricading my mouth shut
for fear of letting anything less than masterpiece
get mud on the rug.
My fear took the fire in my heart and held it to my throat,
daring me to tempt it,

So I wrote this poem.

I don't know why this show called life
keeps getting renewed for another season,
but I do know that my lungs don't feel as heavy
while I'm singing.
In the hardest times, I sit plucking the tattoos on my brain
like guitar strings
and playing them on full blast,
no matter the sound.

We're in Italy.
Follow me through the Blue Grotto
and watch all the lights flitter and dance along the cave
walls like the stranger I held
in a pizza shop the last night of our trip.
Here, I feel like I could open my mouth

and remember the great-grandmother I never got the chance
to meet,
as if I could drink in all the stories she loved to tell, like
how she would go on for an hour about how kind
the paper boy was or the movie she loved as a kid but
could never remember the name of.

Or I could talk about a stretch of highway
turned laser light show by ambulance
the night a married couple drove headfirst into
oncoming traffic
leaving the dive bar I worked as a teenager.
The pulse of the wind swept them off their bar stools
and carried them straight into the mouth of God.
A motorcycle in a pool of its own blood,
their only receipt for the evening.

All of this is to say that I know how fragile this life can be.
I sat home, unemployed,
after my fifth brain surgery in two years.
And as the doctor vacuumed the blood from my skull like
wine on shag carpeting,
I watched as every microphone and pen in my desk
drawer
faded into mist.

it's a scary thing, those 2am wake up calls,
not knowing where you are
or what your name is.
Every clock in every hospital room is draped in cherry skin,
Bittersweet.
Every second sour
like the friend who lives too far away to come visit
or the loved ones who didn't even know you were sick.

I walk into my first open mic after coming home
and see my fear sitting right there in the front row,

looking me dead in the face.
"Feeling brave?" he asks.
Before I start my set I order a drink from the bar.
Vodka and lemonade with a twist,
just the way I like it.
I raise my glass and see
all the smiles in the audience.
And then there's him.

"Here's to us," I say.
"I'm so glad you all could make it."

<u>Discharge</u>   2022

Three surgeries in one week,
Yeah, the last year's been serious.
But not even anesthesia could make me feel delirious.
You thought that I'd fold with the cards I was dealt,
but I run the house and I bet on myself.

Don't tell me that I got no reason to tell ya
I earned it.
I used to think I was a failure.
I never felt worthy of all this regalia
but now I'm so fancy like Iggy Azalea.

I'm so fancy ♪♩♫

Nurses took me on rooftop to look at the city,
I'm loving the lights, they're all looking so pretty.
Alone in this room but I know God is with me.
I'm gonna get out of this hospital quickly.

*"Mr. Snaman, we're going to need to keep you here and
monitor your progress for the next few days
to make sure everything is working the way it's supposed
to."*

Son of a…

Okay, maybe not quickly, but sooner or later,
I'm gonna be back in my bed, simply laid up.
Lay up like Curry, my enemies scurry
even though my vision's still looking real blurry.

I bury my doubts, someone call the preacher.
I need to get back to my life as a teacher.
These kids said they need ya to reach 'em like Caesar.

Not Julius, the one that be feeding me pizza.

So please take me home. We can dance in confetti.
I'm starving, let's go and get us some spaghetti.
I'm riding this wave and just want to say,
I pray that my readers will never forget me.

42

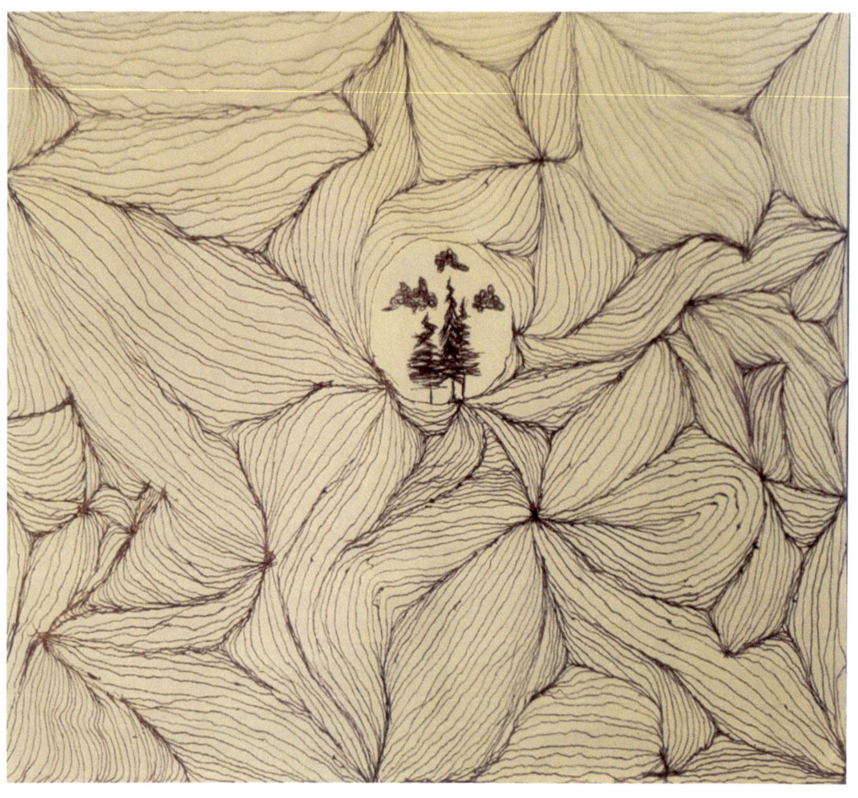

www.ingramcontent.com/pod-product-compliance
Lightning Source LLC
Chambersburg PA
CBHW040946110726
48006CB00007B/1283